Lessons Learned

The Practical Guide for Your Life Lessons

ISBN: 978-0-578-45356-9

Library of Congress Control Number: 2019901463

First Edition, 2019

Dedication

_____

_____

_____

_____

_____

_____

_____

_____

_____

_____

A Note from Michael Thomas

I have always had a strong desire to compile the lessons that I have learned growing up so that one day I could pass them on to my children. I had the fear that if I passed away tomorrow without recording it, all of those years of experience would be lost for the next generation to figure out on their own. I have great aspirations for the futures of my loved ones and hope that they grow to be all that they are capable of being.

The best teachers are ones that can take a complex topic and convey it in simple understandable terms. While we can convey our lessons for each value in academic, idealistic, and theoretical terms, all of which are important, sometimes what is the most helpful is clear advice that can be directly applied to situations that we face daily. That is the difference between ideas and guidance. The goal that I have for my personal book is to boil down what can be confusing, intricate topics and deliver them into simple meaningful messages.

For example if you ask someone to explain love, most people will find it difficult and usually you will not get a definition that helps you find love. However, my grandfather had three simple things to say about love that helped me put it into perspective. "Love needs three things" he would say, "The physical connection, the mental connection, and the social connection. You need to be attracted to each other to be interested, you need to be on the same level mentally to communicate well, and you need to enjoy doing similar types of activities to enjoy and spend time together." He would joke and say "a couple can get by fine with just two of the connections, but if you only have one, you might be in trouble."

There are so many things in this world that we encounter as we mature, lessons that are both big and small. Even if we are not around to convey each lesson personally, if we record the most important ones, we will have the assurance that we have left real direction that will help our loved ones for years to come. If we are lucky, they don't have to learn every lesson the hard way but can learn based on what we teach them.

What is special about this book is that it allows the author to convey each topic their way. This is what will be cherished by the writer's loved ones more than anything. Hopefully, the writer's audience will have more than a keepsake but a book which will provide them guidance to thrive for years to come. Additionally, it can help memorialize the writer's personality and vision. I have found this book very helpful. It has provided me with some comfort that once I am gone, I will still be able to help my family when they need it. I hope you do too.

Preface

Lessons Learned is the guide that provides you with a template to compile your life lessons in an eloquent, direct, and helpful manner for your audience. The format provided outlines life's decisive components and while the book does not exhaust of all life's nuances, it provides a high level outline for life's most pertinent aspects. It allows you, the writer, to record and organize practical guidance of your most cherished values to pass on to your loved ones.

Life is not easy, we all face challenges during our lifetime. With shared wisdom and strong values to provide a solid foundation, we can avoid the pitfalls and road blocks that arise throughout life. Understanding life's components and being equipped with the knowledge to make the most informed decisions, we may grow to our full potential.

Only you can convey what principles have been most valuable to you during your life, and how best to apply them. How they will be interpreted by your audience will be based on how you describe your experiences. Your narrative to each section will bring the most meaning to your ideals, morals, and values. Record your lessons so that when your loved ones need guidance, they can refer to your words.

Not one of us are exactly alike, and we do not hold all the same principles or attach the same importance to each principle. Therefore, Lessons Learned allows for customization by the author. This includes blank templates to be filled out which includes family history, an author's narrative, lessons learned, a book list and a quote list.

The book has been broken into eight sections to provide an effective template for you to describe the most important lessons you have learned and applied during your life. The goal is to provide a reference manual for your audience to help guide them to the best decisions they can make throughout their life.

The Format of Lessons Learned

Lesson's Learned has been divided into eight sections. Each section provides a framework for the author to compile their narrative to the respective subject. The roles of each section are described below:

Section A - Family History

Knowing our family history provides the context of our lives. It highlights where we came from and breeds an appreciation for our current situation. The first section is geared towards describing your family's relationships, their history, and anecdotal information about the members of the author's family.

Popular Additions: When/where born, marriage, occupation, where resided, children, life events, personality traits, favorite pass times.

Section B – Author's Narrative

The narrative section provides an area for the author to introduce their perspective. This is to provide better context for the author's readers and allow the author to provide the proper setting of their life lessons.

Popular Additions: Autobiographical information, challenges and accomplishments, life priorities, wishes for your loved ones.

Section C – Lessons Learned

The Lessons Learned section outlines subjects for the author to narrate. The section provides a guide for the author to convey to their audience the importance of the given topic in a way which can enhance the reader's life, while revealing to the reader the author's character, beliefs, and life. Twelve pages are provided with blank headings for the author to provide their own subjects as they see necessary.

Popular Additions: Stories, memories, teachings, instructions, situational tips, examples.

Section D - Addenda

Throughout our lives we always add to our knowledge as we grow through new experiences. Included is an addenda section to allow the author to expand on their previously written work. At the bottom of relevant pages, a line for addenda is provided. When the author would like to direct their reader to the Addenda section, the author simply writes the page number of the respective addenda section they would like their reader to refer to. Multiple Addenda pages may be referenced by providing a comma between page numbers on the addenda line.

Section E – Family Recipes

Every family has dishes that when eaten, make us feel like we are home. Our family recipes provide us with more than nutrition or a sweet treat, they remind us of our heritage and help us bond with our family. This section has been provided so that the author can pass on their favorite family recipes.

Section F – Influential Books

The importance of reading cannot be understated. Books influence our knowledge and understanding of life. Reading provides us with an education beyond what we can see. They can deliver the information necessary for the success of our endeavors and provide hours of entertainment. For many circumstances, we may like to recommend books to our loved ones. This section is provided to relay helpful books to the audience and what books have been most inspirational and influential in the author's life.

Section G – Helpful Quotes

Quotes can be inspirational, educational, and comical. They can summarize briefly important life lessons which reflect our experiences. This section is provided for the author to share their favorite quotes that have helped them through their lives.

Section H – Hierarchy of Needs

The Hierarchy of Needs is provided as a reference for the audience. The first step towards self-improvement is to be aware of the stages of development and understand our current situation. Providing the knowledge and context of our needs, allows us to objectively evaluate who we are and who we want to be.

Lessons Learned is formatted to provide a personalized book tailored to the author's tastes. To further customize the book for your audience, once you are comfortable with the format of the book, remove the pages with the dashed lines including; A Note from Michael Thomas, the Preface, and The Format of Lessons Learned.

TABLE OF CONTENTS

SECTION A – FAMILY HISTORY

Family Tree – Maternal Heritage

Parent's Name
Parent's Additional Sibling
etc.

Family Tree – Paternal Heritage

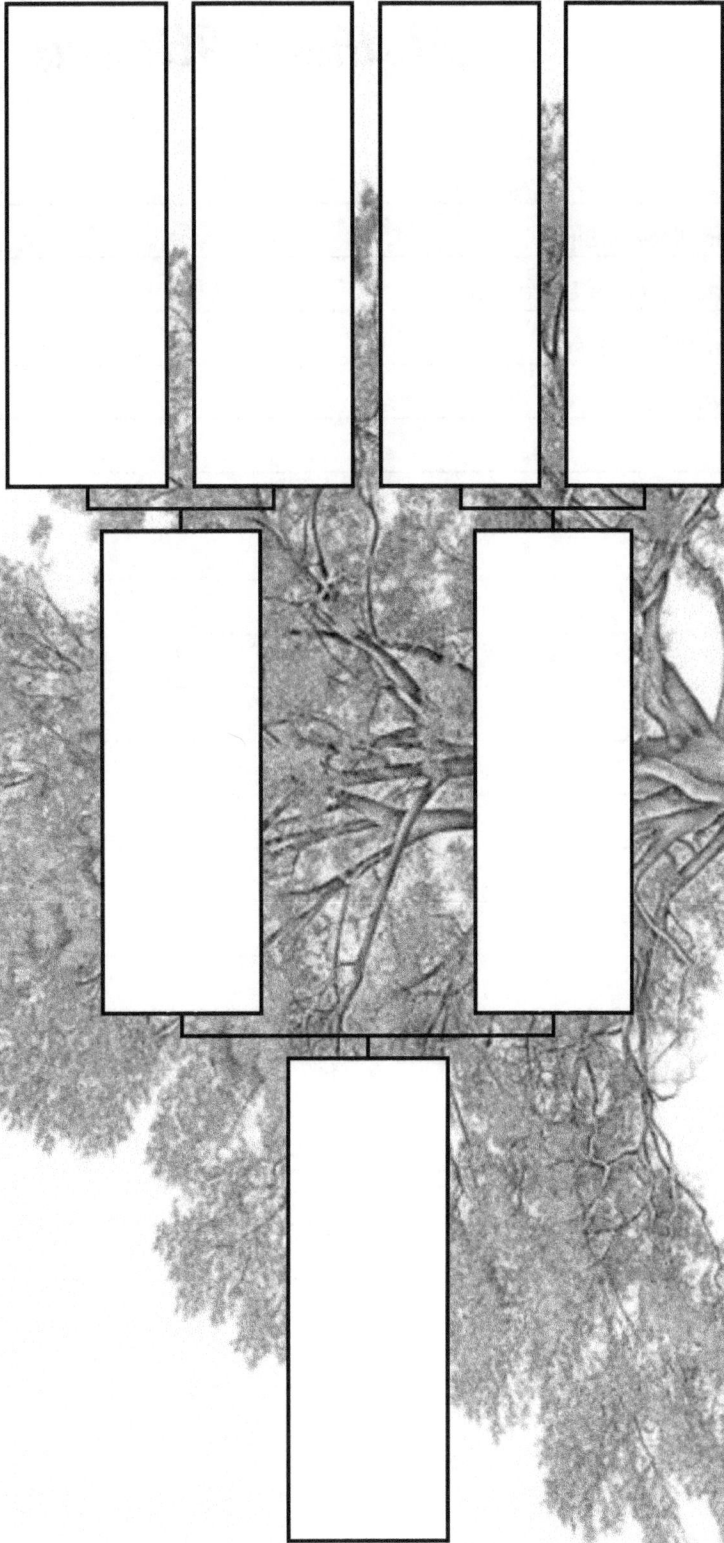

Mother's History

Name: _____

Date and Place of Birth: _____

Date and Place of Deceased: _____

Location of Remains: _____

Narrative: _____

_____

_____

_____

_____

_____

_____

_____

_____

_____

_____

_____

_____

_____

_____

_____

_____

_____

_____

_____

Addenda: _____

_____

Father's History

Name: _____

Date and Place of Birth: _____

Date and Place of Deceased: _____

Location of Remains: _____

Narrative: _____

_____
_____
_____
_____
_____
_____
_____
_____
_____
_____
_____
_____
_____
_____
_____
_____
_____
_____
_____
_____
_____
_____

Addenda: _____

Siblings' History

Name: _____

Date and Place of Birth: _____

Date and Place of Deceased: _____

Location of Remains: _____

Narrative: _____

_____

_____

_____

_____

_____

_____

_____

_____

Name: _____

Date and Place of Birth: _____

Date and Place of Deceased: _____

Location of Remains: _____

Narrative: _____

_____

_____

_____

_____

_____

_____

_____

Addenda: _____

Siblings' History Continued

Name: _____

Date and Place of Birth: _____

Date and Place of Deceased: _____

Location of Remains: _____

Narrative: _____

_____

_____

_____

_____

_____

_____

_____

Name: _____

Date and Place of Birth: _____

Date and Place of Deceased: _____

Location of Remains: _____

Narrative: _____

_____

_____

_____

_____

_____

_____

_____

Addenda: _____

My Maternal Grandparents' History

Name: _____

Date and Place of Birth: _____

Date and Place of Deceased: _____

Location of Remains: _____

Narrative: _____

_____

_____

_____

_____

_____

_____

_____

_____

_____

Name: _____

Date and Place of Birth: _____

Date and Place of Deceased: _____

Location of Remains: _____

Narrative: _____

_____

_____

_____

_____

_____

_____

_____

Addenda: _____

My Paternal Grandparents' History

Name: _____

Date and Place of Birth: _____

Date and Place of Deceased: _____

Location of Remains: _____

Narrative: _____

_____

_____

_____

_____

_____

_____

_____

_____

Name: _____

Date and Place of Birth: _____

Date and Place of Deceased: _____

Location of Remains: _____

Narrative: _____

_____

_____

_____

_____

_____

_____

_____

Addenda: _____

My Maternal Great-Grandparents' History

Name: _____

Date and Place of Birth: _____

Date and Place of Deceased: _____

Location of Remains: _____

Narrative: _____

_____

_____

_____

_____

_____

_____

_____

_____

_____

Name: _____

Date and Place of Birth: _____

Date and Place of Deceased: _____

Location of Remains: _____

Narrative: _____

_____

_____

_____

_____

_____

_____

_____

Addenda: _____

My Maternal Great-Grandparents' History Continued

Name: _____

Date and Place of Birth: _____

Date and Place of Deceased: _____

Location of Remains: _____

Narrative: _____

_____

_____

_____

_____

_____

_____

_____

Name: _____

Date and Place of Birth: _____

Date and Place of Deceased: _____

Location of Remains: _____

Narrative: _____

_____

_____

_____

_____

_____

_____

Addenda: _____

My Paternal Great-Grandparents' History

Name: _____

Date and Place of Birth: _____

Date and Place of Deceased: _____

Location of Remains: _____

Narrative: _____

_____

_____

_____

_____

_____

_____

_____

_____

_____

Name: _____

Date and Place of Birth: _____

Date and Place of Deceased: _____

Location of Remains: _____

Narrative: _____

_____

_____

_____

_____

_____

_____

Addenda: _____

_____

My Paternal Great-Grandparents'
History Continued

Name: _____

Date and Place of Birth: _____

Date and Place of Deceased: _____

Location of Remains: _____

Narrative: _____

_____

_____

_____

_____

_____

_____

Name: _____

Date and Place of Birth: _____

Date and Place of Deceased: _____

Location of Remains: _____

Narrative: _____

_____

_____

_____

_____

_____

Addenda: _____

Additional Family

Name: _____

Date and Place of Birth: _____

Date and Place of Deceased: _____

Location of Remains: _____

Narrative: _____

_____

_____

_____

_____

_____

_____

_____

_____

Name: _____

Date and Place of Birth: _____

Date and Place of Deceased: _____

Location of Remains: _____

Narrative: _____

_____

_____

_____

_____

_____

_____

Addenda: _____

Additional Family

Name: _____

Date and Place of Birth: _____

Date and Place of Deceased: _____

Location of Remains: _____

Narrative: _____

_____

_____

_____

_____

_____

_____

_____

_____

Name: _____

Date and Place of Birth: _____

Date and Place of Deceased: _____

Location of Remains: _____

Narrative: _____

_____

_____

_____

_____

_____

_____

_____

Addenda: _____

Additional Family

Name: _____

Date and Place of Birth: _____

Date and Place of Deceased: _____

Location of Remains: _____

Narrative: _____

_____

_____

_____

_____

_____

_____

_____

_____

Name: _____

Date and Place of Birth: _____

Date and Place of Deceased: _____

Location of Remains: _____

Narrative: _____

_____

_____

_____

_____

_____

_____

_____

Addenda: _____

Pets

Name: _____ Years: _____

Type of Animal: _____ Narrative: _____

_____

_____

Name: _____ Years: _____

Type of Animal: _____ Narrative: _____

_____

_____

Name: _____ Years: _____

Type of Animal: _____ Narrative: _____

_____

_____

Name: _____ Years: _____

Type of Animal: _____ Narrative: _____

_____

_____

Name: _____ Years: _____

Type of Animal: _____ Narrative: _____

_____

_____

Addenda: _____

Family Traditions

_____
_____
_____
_____
_____
_____
_____
_____
_____
_____
_____
_____
_____
_____
_____
_____
_____
_____
_____
_____
_____
_____
_____
_____
_____

Addenda: _____

Heirlooms

_____
_____
_____
_____
_____
_____
_____
_____
_____
_____
_____
_____
_____
_____
_____
_____
_____
_____
_____
_____
_____
_____
_____
_____

Addenda:
_____

SECTION B – AUTHOR'S NARRATIVE

Narrative from the Author

_____
_____
_____
_____
_____
_____
_____
_____
_____
_____
_____
_____
_____
_____
_____
_____
_____
_____
_____
_____
_____

Addenda: _____

Addenda:

Addenda:

Addenda:

Addenda: _____

Addenda:

Addenda:

Addenda:

Addenda: _____

Addenda:

SECTION C – LESSONS LEARNED

Reference List:

- ☐ Achievement
- ☐ Adventure
- ☐ Appearance
- ☐ Appreciation
- ☐ Attitude
- ☐ Brooding
- ☐ Change
- ☐ Compassion
- ☐ Confidence
- ☐ Courage
- ☐ Creativity
- ☐ Critics
- ☐ Culture
- ☐ Curiosity
- ☐ Determination
- ☐ Diet
- ☐ Discipline
- ☐ Discouragement
- ☐ Drugs
- ☐ Education
- ☐ Faith
- ☐ Family
- ☐ Finance
- ☐ Friendship

- ☐ Giving
- ☐ Gratitude
- ☐ Growth
- ☐ Habits
- ☐ Happiness
- ☐ Harmony
- ☐ Health
- ☐ Honesty
- ☐ Humor
- ☐ Intuition
- ☐ Integrity
- ☐ Leadership
- ☐ Life
- ☐ Love
- ☐ Loyalty
- ☐ Luck
- ☐ Morals
- ☐ Music and Dance
- ☐ Optimism
- ☐ Parenting
- ☐ Physical Fitness
- ☐ Planning
- ☐ Politics
- ☐ Recognition

- ☐ Religion
- ☐ Reputation
- ☐ Resentment
- ☐ Respect
- ☐ Responsibility
- ☐ Self-Help
- ☐ Self-Respect
- ☐ Sports
- ☐ Stress
- ☐ Time
- ☐ Wealth
- ☐ Work
- ☐ _____
- ☐ _____
- ☐ _____
- ☐ _____
- ☐ _____
- ☐ _____
- ☐ _____
- ☐ _____
- ☐ _____
- ☐ _____
- ☐ _____
- ☐ _____

ACHIEVEMENT

Success comes down to attitude and determination.

_____
_____
_____
_____
_____
_____
_____
_____
_____
_____
_____
_____
_____
_____
_____
_____
_____
_____
_____
_____

Addenda: _____

ADVENTURE

Big and small, new activities provide for great fun and memories.

_____

_____

_____

_____

_____

_____

_____

_____

_____

_____

_____

_____

_____

_____

_____

_____

_____

_____

_____

_____

_____

_____

_____

Addenda: _____

APPEARANCE

We all want to project an image we feel good about, but it is far from our most important trait.

_____

_____

_____

_____

_____

_____

_____

_____

_____

_____

_____

_____

_____

_____

_____

_____

_____

_____

_____

_____

_____

Addenda: _____

_____

APPRECIATION

"The day you trade expectation for appreciation is the day you become wealthy."

- Tony Robbins

_____

_____

_____

_____

_____

_____

_____

_____

_____

_____

_____

_____

_____

_____

_____

_____

_____

_____

_____

_____

Addenda: _____

ATTITUDE

"Some people want it to happen, some wish it would happen, others make it happen"

– Michael Jordan

_____

_____

_____

_____

_____

_____

_____

_____

_____

_____

_____

_____

_____

_____

_____

_____

_____

_____

_____

Addenda:

BROODING

When you dwell on an issue, you only waste time you could use to help solve your problem.

_____

_____

_____

_____

_____

_____

_____

_____

_____

_____

_____

_____

_____

_____

_____

_____

_____

_____

_____

_____

_____

_____

Addenda: _____

CHANGE

The world is constantly changing, to thrive, we must change with it.

_____
_____
_____
_____
_____
_____
_____
_____
_____
_____
_____
_____
_____
_____
_____
_____
_____
_____
_____
_____
_____
_____
_____

Addenda:
_____

COMPASSION

"If your compassion does not include yourself, it is incomplete."

- Buddha

_____

_____

_____

_____

_____

_____

_____

_____

_____

_____

_____

_____

_____

_____

_____

_____

_____

_____

_____

_____

Addenda: _____

CONFIDENCE

The self-assurance that you are important and competent.

_____
_____
_____
_____
_____
_____
_____
_____
_____
_____
_____
_____
_____
_____
_____
_____
_____
_____
_____

Addenda: _____

COURAGE

When life presents you with a challenge, have the courage to face it and overcome it.

_____

_____

_____

_____

_____

_____

_____

_____

_____

_____

_____

_____

_____

_____

_____

_____

_____

_____

_____

_____

Addenda: _____

CREATIVITY

Your ally in problem solving.

_____
_____
_____
_____
_____
_____
_____
_____
_____
_____
_____
_____
_____
_____
_____
_____
_____
_____
_____
_____
_____

Addenda:
_____

CRITICS

It's nice to have people like you, but it's a skill to not care about the thoughts

of those you don't care about.

_____

_____

_____

_____

_____

_____

_____

_____

_____

_____

_____

_____

_____

_____

_____

_____

_____

_____

_____

_____

Addenda:
_____

CULTURE

The knowledge and understanding of the things that people in a particular group enjoy and value.

_____

_____

_____

_____

_____

_____

_____

_____

_____

_____

_____

_____

_____

_____

_____

_____

_____

_____

Addenda:
_____

CURIOSITY

Leave no stone unturned.

_____

_____

_____

_____

_____

_____

_____

_____

_____

_____

_____

_____

_____

_____

_____

_____

_____

_____

_____

_____

Addenda:
_____

DETERMINATION

"Doing what needs to be done even when you don't feel like doing it."

- Unknown

_____

_____

_____

_____

_____

_____

_____

_____

_____

_____

_____

_____

_____

_____

_____

_____

_____

_____

_____

_____

_____

Addenda: _____

DIET

A healthy diet leads to a healthy body and mind.

_____

_____

_____

_____

_____

_____

_____

_____

_____

_____

_____

_____

_____

_____

_____

_____

_____

_____

_____

_____

Addenda:
_____

DISCIPLINE

"The price of discipline is always less than the pain of regret"

- Nido R. Qubien

_____

_____

_____

_____

_____

_____

_____

_____

_____

_____

_____

_____

_____

_____

_____

_____

_____

_____

_____

_____

_____

Addenda: _____

DISCOURAGEMENT

Everyone falls down during their life, it is how they get back up that matters.

_____
_____
_____
_____
_____
_____
_____
_____
_____
_____
_____
_____
_____
_____
_____
_____
_____
_____
_____

Addenda:

DRUGS

Life is hard enough. You don't need to create more problems for yourself.

_____

_____

_____

_____

_____

_____

_____

_____

_____

_____

_____

_____

_____

_____

_____

_____

_____

Addenda: _____

EDUCATION

"There are two educations. One should teach us how to make a living and the other how to live."

— John Adams

_____

_____

_____

_____

_____

_____

_____

_____

_____

_____

_____

_____

_____

_____

_____

_____

_____

_____

_____

Addenda: _____

FAITH

"Your faith can move mountains and your doubt can make them."

- Unknown

_____
_____
_____
_____
_____
_____
_____
_____
_____
_____
_____
_____
_____
_____
_____
_____
_____
_____

Addenda:

FAMILY

"You don't choose your family, they are god's gift to you as you are to them."

— Desmond Tutu

_____

Addenda: _____

FINANCE

"Is not merely about making money. It's about achieving our deep goals and protecting the fruits of our labor." – Robert Shiller

_____
_____
_____
_____
_____
_____
_____
_____
_____
_____
_____
_____
_____
_____
_____
_____
_____
_____
_____
_____
_____

Addenda:
_____

FRIENDSHIP

Friendship enriches your life.

_____

_____

_____

_____

_____

_____

_____

_____

_____

_____

_____

_____

_____

_____

_____

_____

_____

_____

_____

Addenda: _____

GIVING

"We make a living by what we get, we make a life by what we give."

– Winston Churchill.

_____

_____

_____

_____

_____

_____

_____

_____

_____

_____

_____

_____

_____

_____

_____

_____

_____

_____

_____

_____

Addenda: _____

GRATITUDE

"If you want to find happiness, find gratitude."

— Steve Maraboli

_____

_____

_____

_____

_____

_____

_____

_____

_____

_____

_____

_____

_____

_____

_____

_____

_____

_____

_____

_____

_____

Addenda: _____

GROWTH

"Be not afraid of growing slowly, but only of standing still."

– Chinese Proverb

_____

_____

_____

_____

_____

_____

_____

_____

_____

_____

_____

_____

_____

_____

_____

_____

_____

_____

_____

_____

_____

Addenda: _____

HABITS

They can be helpful or hurtful, they are learned and can be unlearned.

_____
_____
_____
_____
_____
_____
_____
_____
_____
_____
_____
_____
_____
_____
_____
_____
_____
_____
_____
_____

Addenda: _____

HAPPINESS

Find your joy in each day.

_____

_____

_____

_____

_____

_____

_____

_____

_____

_____

_____

_____

_____

_____

_____

_____

_____

_____

Addenda:

HARMONY

"Happiness is when what you think, what you say, and what you do are in harmony."

— Mohatma Gandhi

_____

_____

_____

_____

_____

_____

_____

_____

_____

_____

_____

_____

_____

_____

_____

_____

_____

_____

_____

_____

Addenda:

HEALTH

"An ounce of prevention is worth a pound of cure."

- Benjamin Franklin

_____
_____
_____
_____
_____
_____
_____
_____
_____
_____
_____
_____
_____
_____
_____
_____
_____
_____
_____
_____

Addenda: _____

HONESTY

To be proud of yourself and keep your conscious clear.

_____
_____
_____
_____
_____
_____
_____
_____
_____
_____
_____
_____
_____
_____
_____
_____
_____
_____
_____

Addenda:
_____

HUMOR

To keep life light, enjoy the humor in everything.

_____

_____

_____

_____

_____

_____

_____

_____

_____

_____

_____

_____

_____

_____

_____

_____

_____

_____

_____

Addenda: _____

INTUITION

Our intuition is our subconscious directing us based on our memories we can't immediately recall.

_____
_____
_____
_____
_____
_____
_____
_____
_____
_____
_____
_____
_____
_____
_____
_____
_____
_____
_____
_____

Addenda:

INTEGRITY

"Choosing your thoughts and actions based on values rather than personal gain."

– Chris Karcher

_____
_____
_____
_____
_____
_____
_____
_____
_____
_____
_____
_____
_____
_____
_____
_____
_____
_____
_____
_____
_____
_____

Addenda:
_____

LEADERSHIP

"A leader is one who knows the way, goes the way, and shows the way."

— John Maxwell

_____

_____

_____

_____

_____

_____

_____

_____

_____

_____

_____

_____

_____

_____

_____

_____

_____

_____

_____

_____

_____

_____

Addenda: _____

LIFE

Time goes by either way; live life, be happy.

_____

_____

_____

_____

_____

_____

_____

_____

_____

_____

_____

_____

_____

_____

_____

_____

_____

Addenda: _____

LOVE

Love provides the warmth in your life.

_____

_____

_____

_____

_____

_____

_____

_____

_____

_____

_____

_____

_____

_____

_____

_____

_____

_____

_____

_____

_____

_____

Addenda:
_____

LOYALTY

Devotion towards what you feel is important.

_____
_____
_____
_____
_____
_____
_____
_____
_____
_____
_____
_____
_____
_____
_____
_____
_____
_____
_____

Addenda: _____

LUCK

Where preparation meets opportunity.

_____
_____
_____
_____
_____
_____
_____
_____
_____
_____
_____
_____
_____
_____
_____
_____
_____
_____
_____
_____

Addenda: _____

MORALS

The basis for your thoughts, actions, and results.

_____
_____
_____
_____
_____
_____
_____
_____
_____
_____
_____
_____
_____
_____
_____
_____
_____
_____
_____
_____
_____

Addenda: _____

MUSIC & DANCE

Some people listen to music like they wear a fashion, just enjoy what you like.

Addenda:

OPTIMISM

Whether the glass is half empty or half full, it means the same thing, but with what outlook are you happier?

_____
_____
_____
_____
_____
_____
_____
_____
_____
_____
_____
_____
_____
_____
_____
_____
_____
_____
_____
_____
_____
_____

Addenda:

PARENTING

Life's most fulfilling joy.

_____

_____

_____

_____

_____

_____

_____

_____

_____

_____

_____

_____

_____

_____

_____

_____

_____

_____

_____

Addenda:
_____

PHYSICAL FITNESS

To have energy, you need to be active.

_____
_____
_____
_____
_____
_____
_____
_____
_____
_____
_____
_____
_____
_____
_____
_____
_____
_____
_____
_____

Addenda: _____

PLANNING

The days go by either way, plan for your future to improve your current situation.

Addenda:

POLITICS

The process of choosing decisions through cooperation with others.

_____
_____
_____
_____
_____
_____
_____
_____
_____
_____
_____
_____
_____
_____
_____
_____
_____
_____
_____
_____
_____

Addenda:

RECOGNITION

Innately we all like to be valued.

_____

_____

_____

_____

_____

_____

_____

_____

_____

_____

_____

_____

_____

_____

_____

_____

_____

_____

_____

Addenda: _____

RELIGION

For culture, practices, behavior, and spirituality.

_____
_____
_____
_____
_____
_____
_____
_____
_____
_____
_____
_____
_____
_____
_____
_____
_____
_____
_____
_____
_____

Addenda:
_____

REPUTATION

The world is small, how do you want to be perceived?

_____
_____
_____
_____
_____
_____
_____
_____
_____
_____
_____
_____
_____
_____
_____
_____
_____
_____
_____

Addenda:

RESENTMENT

"Don't hold a grudge or a chip and here's why, bitterness keeps you from flying"

– Tim McGraw

_____

_____

_____

_____

_____

_____

_____

_____

_____

_____

_____

_____

_____

_____

_____

_____

_____

_____

_____

_____

Addenda: _____

RESPECT

Usually, people give you what you give them.

_____

_____

_____

_____

_____

_____

_____

_____

_____

_____

_____

_____

_____

_____

_____

_____

_____

_____

Addenda:

_____

RESPONSIBILITY

What can you do today, to make your life easier tomorrow?

_____
_____
_____
_____
_____
_____
_____
_____
_____
_____
_____
_____
_____
_____
_____
_____
_____
_____

Addenda: _____

SELF-HELP

To grow is to live. Perhaps the best investment you can make, is in yourself.

_____
_____
_____
_____
_____
_____
_____
_____
_____
_____
_____
_____
_____
_____
_____
_____
_____
_____
_____
_____
_____

Addenda:

SELF-RESPECT

Realize your importance.

_____
_____
_____
_____
_____
_____
_____
_____
_____
_____
_____
_____
_____
_____
_____
_____
_____
_____
_____
_____

Addenda:

SPORTS

For fun, competition, exercise, and to learn how to play and work well with others.

_____
_____
_____
_____
_____
_____
_____
_____
_____
_____
_____
_____
_____
_____
_____
_____
_____
_____
_____
_____
_____

Addenda: _____

STRESS

Can be good and bad but either way, needs to be managed.

_____

_____

_____

_____

_____

_____

_____

_____

_____

_____

_____

_____

_____

_____

_____

_____

_____

_____

_____

_____

_____

Addenda:
_____

TIME

Your most precious resource, make every day count.

_____
_____
_____
_____
_____
_____
_____
_____
_____
_____
_____
_____
_____
_____
_____
_____
_____
_____
_____
_____

Addenda: _____

WEALTH

"The first places to be wealthy are psychologically, emotionally, and spiritually"

- Tony Robbins

_____
_____
_____
_____
_____
_____
_____
_____
_____
_____
_____
_____
_____
_____
_____
_____
_____
_____
_____
_____

Addenda:
_____

WORK

Work smart, not hard.

_____
_____
_____
_____
_____
_____
_____
_____
_____
_____
_____
_____
_____
_____
_____
_____
_____
_____
_____

Addenda:

Addenda:

_____

_____
_____
_____
_____
_____
_____
_____
_____
_____
_____
_____
_____
_____
_____
_____
_____
_____
_____
_____
_____
_____
_____

Addenda: _____

_____

_____
_____
_____
_____
_____
_____
_____
_____
_____
_____
_____
_____
_____
_____
_____
_____
_____
_____
_____
_____
_____
_____
_____

Addenda:
_____

_____

_____
_____
_____
_____
_____
_____
_____
_____
_____
_____
_____
_____
_____
_____
_____
_____
_____
_____
_____
_____
_____

Addenda: _____

_____

_____
_____
_____
_____
_____
_____
_____
_____
_____
_____
_____
_____
_____
_____
_____
_____
_____
_____
_____
_____
_____
_____

Addenda: _____

_____

_____
_____
_____
_____
_____
_____
_____
_____
_____
_____
_____
_____
_____
_____
_____
_____
_____
_____
_____
_____
_____
_____

Addenda: _____

_____

_____
_____
_____
_____
_____
_____
_____
_____
_____
_____
_____
_____
_____
_____
_____
_____
_____
_____
_____
_____
_____
_____
_____
_____

Addenda: _____

_____

_____
_____
_____
_____
_____
_____
_____
_____
_____
_____
_____
_____
_____
_____
_____
_____
_____
_____
_____

Addenda:
_____

_____

_____
_____
_____
_____
_____
_____
_____
_____
_____
_____
_____
_____
_____
_____
_____
_____
_____
_____
_____
_____

Addenda: _____

_____

_____
_____
_____
_____
_____
_____
_____
_____
_____
_____
_____
_____
_____
_____
_____
_____
_____
_____
_____
_____

Addenda: _____

_____

_____
_____
_____
_____
_____
_____
_____
_____
_____
_____
_____
_____
_____
_____
_____
_____
_____
_____
_____
_____

Addenda: _____

_____

_____
_____
_____
_____
_____
_____
_____
_____
_____
_____
_____
_____
_____
_____
_____
_____
_____
_____
_____
_____
_____
_____

Addenda: _____

SECTION D – ADDENDA

Addenda

Section Referenced: _____ Page Number: _____

Addition(s): _____

_____

_____

_____

_____

_____

_____

_____

_____

_____

_____

Section Referenced: _____ Page Number: _____

Addition(s): _____

_____

_____

_____

_____

_____

_____

_____

_____

_____

_____

Section Referenced: _____   Page Number: _____

Addition(s): _____

_____

_____

_____

_____

_____

_____

_____

_____

_____

_____

_____

Section Referenced: _____   Page Number: _____

Addition(s): _____

_____

_____

_____

_____

_____

_____

_____

_____

_____

_____

_____

Section Referenced: _____ Page Number: _____

Addition(s): _____

_____

_____

_____

_____

_____

_____

_____

_____

_____

_____

_____

Section Referenced: _____ Page Number: _____

Addition(s): _____

_____

_____

_____

_____

_____

_____

_____

_____

_____

_____

_____

Section Referenced: _____   Page Number: _____

Addition(s): _____

_____

_____

_____

_____

_____

_____

_____

_____

_____

_____

Section Referenced: _____   Page Number: _____

Addition(s): _____

_____

_____

_____

_____

_____

_____

_____

_____

_____

_____

Section Referenced: _____ Page Number: _____

Addition(s): _____

_____

_____

_____

_____

_____

_____

_____

_____

_____

_____

_____

_____

Section Referenced: _____ Page Number: _____

Addition(s): _____

_____

_____

_____

_____

_____

_____

_____

_____

_____

_____

_____

_____

_____

Section Referenced: _____ Page Number: _____

Addition(s): _____

_____

_____

_____

_____

_____

_____

_____

_____

_____

_____

_____

Section Referenced: _____ Page Number: _____

Addition(s): _____

_____

_____

_____

_____

_____

_____

_____

_____

_____

_____

_____

Section Referenced: _____ Page Number: _____

Addition(s): _____

_____

_____

_____

_____

_____

_____

_____

_____

_____

_____

_____

Section Referenced: _____ Page Number: _____

Addition(s): _____

_____

_____

_____

_____

_____

_____

_____

_____

_____

_____

_____

Section Referenced: _____ Page Number: _____

Addition(s): _____

_____

_____

_____

_____

_____

_____

_____

_____

_____

_____

_____

Section Referenced: _____ Page Number: _____

Addition(s): _____

_____

_____

_____

_____

_____

_____

_____

_____

_____

_____

_____

_____

Section Referenced: _____ Page Number: _____

Addition(s): _____

_____

_____

_____

_____

_____

_____

_____

_____

_____

_____

_____

_____

Section Referenced: _____ Page Number: _____

Addition(s): _____

_____

_____

_____

_____

_____

_____

_____

_____

_____

_____

_____

Section Referenced: _____ Page Number: _____

Addition(s): _____

_____

_____

_____

_____

_____

_____

_____

_____

_____

_____

Section Referenced: _____ Page Number: _____

Addition(s): _____

_____

_____

_____

_____

_____

_____

_____

_____

_____

_____

Section Referenced: _____ Page Number: _____

Addition(s): _____

_____

_____

_____

_____

_____

_____

_____

_____

_____

_____

_____

Section Referenced: _____ Page Number: _____

Addition(s): _____

_____

_____

_____

_____

_____

_____

_____

_____

_____

_____

_____

_____

Section Referenced: _____ Page Number: _____

Addition(s): _____

_____
_____
_____
_____
_____
_____
_____
_____
_____
_____
_____

Section Referenced: _____ Page Number: _____

Addition(s): _____

_____
_____
_____
_____
_____
_____
_____
_____
_____
_____
_____

Section Referenced: _____   Page Number: _____

Addition(s): _____

_____

_____

_____

_____

_____

_____

_____

_____

_____

_____

Section Referenced: _____   Page Number: _____

Addition(s): _____

_____

_____

_____

_____

_____

_____

_____

_____

_____

_____

_____

_____

Section Referenced: _____ Page Number: _____

Addition(s): _____

_____

_____

_____

_____

_____

_____

_____

_____

_____

_____

Section Referenced: _____ Page Number: _____

Addition(s): _____

_____

_____

_____

_____

_____

_____

_____

_____

_____

_____

_____

SECTION E – FAMILY RECIPES

Family Recipes

Recipe: _____   Preparation Time: _____   Serves: _____

Ingredients: _____   _____

_____   _____

_____   _____

_____   _____

Instructions: _____

_____

_____

_____

_____

_____

Recipe: _____   Preparation Time: _____   Serves: _____

Ingredients: _____   _____

_____   _____

_____   _____

_____   _____

Instructions: _____

_____

_____

_____

_____

_____

Recipe: _____   Preparation Time: _____   Serves: _____

Ingredients: _____   _____

_____   _____

_____   _____

_____   _____

_____

Instructions: _____

_____

_____

_____

_____

_____

_____

_____

Recipe: _____   Preparation Time: _____   Serves: _____

Ingredients: _____   _____

_____   _____

_____   _____

_____   _____

Instructions: _____

_____

_____

_____

_____

_____

_____

Recipe: _____   Preparation Time: _____   Serves: _____

Ingredients: _____   _____

_____   _____

_____   _____

_____   _____

_____   _____

Instructions: _____

_____

_____

_____

_____

_____

_____

_____

Recipe: _____   Preparation Time: _____   Serves: _____

Ingredients: _____   _____

_____   _____

_____   _____

_____   _____

_____   _____

Instructions: _____

_____

_____

_____

_____

_____

_____

_____

Recipe: _____   Preparation Time: _____   Serves: _____

Ingredients: _____

_____   _____

_____   _____

_____   _____

_____   _____

Instructions: _____

_____

_____

_____

_____

_____

_____

Recipe: _____   Preparation Time: _____   Serves: _____

Ingredients: _____

_____   _____

_____   _____

_____   _____

_____   _____

Instructions: _____

_____

_____

_____

_____

_____

_____

Recipe: _____ Preparation Time: _____ Serves: _____

Ingredients: _____ _____

_____ _____

_____ _____

_____ _____

_____ _____

Instructions: _____

_____

_____

_____

_____

_____

_____

_____

_____

Recipe: _____ Preparation Time: _____ Serves: _____

Ingredients: _____ _____

_____ _____

_____ _____

_____ _____

Instructions: _____

_____

_____

_____

_____

_____

_____

_____

Recipe: _____ Preparation Time: _____ Serves: _____

Ingredients: _____

_____   _____

_____   _____

_____   _____

_____   _____

Instructions: _____

_____

_____

_____

_____

_____

_____

_____

Recipe: _____ Preparation Time: _____ Serves: _____

Ingredients: _____

_____   _____

_____   _____

_____   _____

_____   _____

Instructions: _____

_____

_____

_____

_____

_____

_____

_____

Recipe: _____ Preparation Time: _____ Serves: _____

Ingredients: _____

_____ _____

_____ _____

_____ _____

_____ _____

Instructions: _____

_____

_____

_____

_____

_____

_____

_____

Recipe: _____ Preparation Time: _____ Serves: _____

Ingredients: _____

_____ _____

_____ _____

_____ _____

_____ _____

Instructions: _____

_____

_____

_____

_____

_____

_____

Recipe: _____   Preparation Time: _____   Serves: _____

Ingredients: _____

_____   _____

_____   _____

_____   _____

_____   _____

Instructions: _____

_____

_____

_____

_____

_____

_____

_____

Recipe: _____   Preparation Time: _____   Serves: _____

Ingredients: _____

_____   _____

_____   _____

_____   _____

_____   _____

Instructions: _____

_____

_____

_____

_____

_____

_____

_____

SECTION F – INFLUENTIAL BOOKS

Book List

Title: _____ Author: _____

Genre: _____ Lesson: _____

_____

Title: _____ Author: _____

Genre: _____ Lesson: _____

_____

Title: _____ Author: _____

Genre: _____ Lesson: _____

_____

Title: _____ Author: _____

Genre: _____ Lesson: _____

_____

Title: _____ Author: _____

Genre: _____ Lesson: _____

_____

Title: _____ Author: _____

Genre: _____ Lesson: _____

_____

Title: _____   Author: _____

Genre: _____   Lesson: _____

_____

Title: _____   Author: _____

Genre: _____   Lesson: _____

_____

Title: _____   Author: _____

Genre: _____   Lesson: _____

_____

Title: _____   Author: _____

Genre: _____   Lesson: _____

_____

Title: _____   Author: _____

Genre: _____   Lesson: _____

_____

Title: _____   Author: _____

Genre: _____   Lesson: _____

_____

Title: _____   Author: _____

Genre: _____   Lesson: _____

_____

Title: _____ Author: _____

Genre: _____ Lesson: _____

_____

Title: _____ Author: _____

Genre: _____ Lesson: _____

_____

Title: _____ Author: _____

Genre: _____ Lesson: _____

_____

Title: _____ Author: _____

Genre: _____ Lesson: _____

_____

Title: _____ Author: _____

Genre: _____ Lesson: _____

_____

Title: _____ Author: _____

Genre: _____ Lesson: _____

_____

Title: _____ Author: _____

Genre: _____ Lesson: _____

_____

Title: _____   Author: _____

Genre: _____   Lesson: _____

_____

Title: _____   Author: _____

Genre: _____   Lesson: _____

_____

Title: _____   Author: _____

Genre: _____   Lesson: _____

_____

Title: _____   Author: _____

Genre: _____   Lesson: _____

_____

Title: _____   Author: _____

Genre: _____   Lesson: _____

_____

Title: _____   Author: _____

Genre: _____   Lesson: _____

_____

Title: _____   Author: _____

Genre: _____   Lesson: _____

_____

SECTION G – HELPFUL QUOTES

Helpful Quotes

SECTION H – HIERARCHY OF NEEDS

Hierarchy of Needs

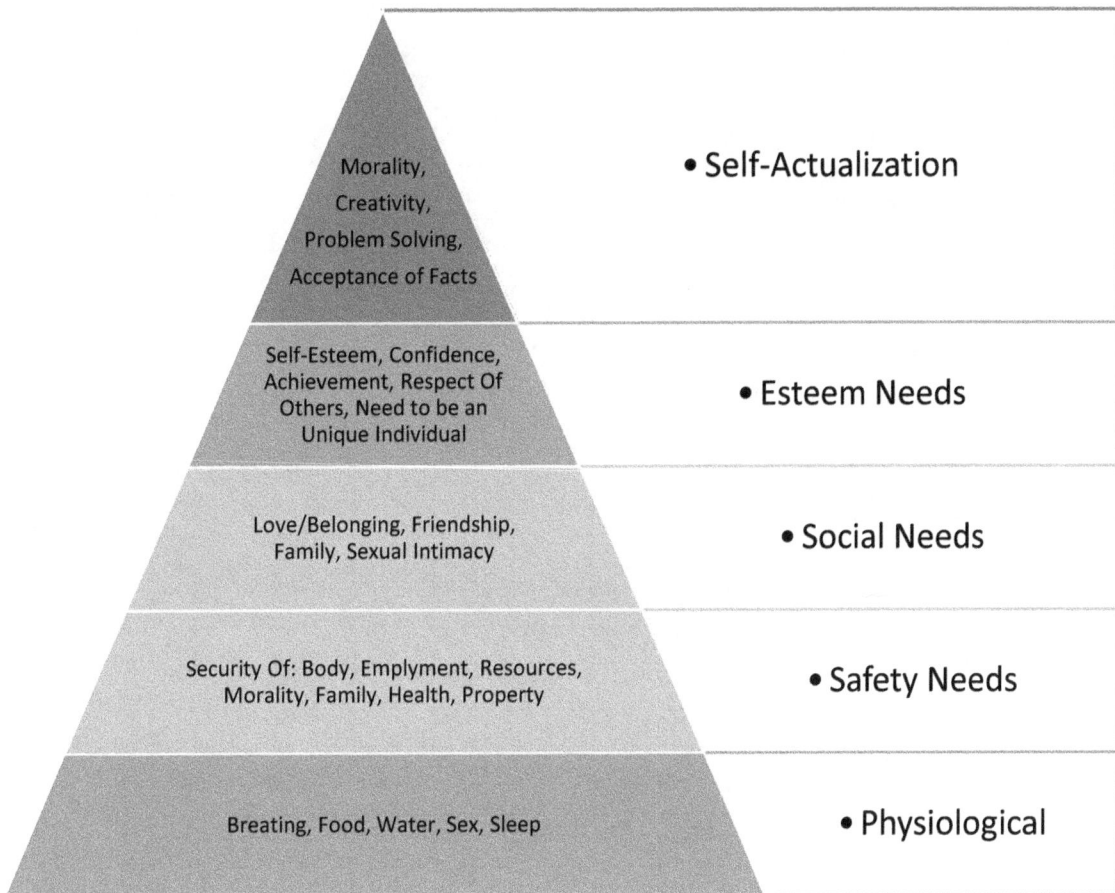

Morality, Creativity, Problem Solving, Acceptance of Facts	• Self-Actualization
Self-Esteem, Confidence, Achievement, Respect Of Others, Need to be an Unique Individual	• Esteem Needs
Love/Belonging, Friendship, Family, Sexual Intimacy	• Social Needs
Security Of: Body, Emplyment, Resources, Morality, Family, Health, Property	• Safety Needs
Breating, Food, Water, Sex, Sleep	• Physiological

Source: Maslow's Hierarchy of Needs